PAPER ANNIVERSARY

Pitt Poetry Series
Ed Ochester, Editor

Paper Anniversary

BOBBY C. ROGERS

To Tom Hanks,

Fellow bird hunter
and lover of literature.
Wonderful to meet your
Waco.

All best,

University of Pittsburgh Press

Published by the University of Pittsburgh Press, Pittsburgh, Pa., 15260

Copyright © 2010, Bobby C. Rogers

All rights reserved

Manufactured in the United States of America

Printed on acid-free paper

10 9 8 7 6 5 4 3 2 1

ISBN 13: 978-0-8229-6124-6

ISBN 10: 0-8229-6124-5

Rebecca

CONTENTS

Small wonder how pitiably we love our home, cling in her skirts at night, rejoice in her wide star-seducing smile, when every star strikes us sick with the fright: do we really exist at all?

—JAMES AGEE, *Let Us Now Praise Famous Men*

PAPER ANNIVERSARY

Meat and Three

Any excuse to knock off work. We love this joint, with its sweet tea and
    pepper sauce,

cornbread in a basket, plate lunch and pie. There's a portrait of Bob the
    owner

over the door: *Eat or we both go hungry*. We seat ourselves, connoisseurs of
    the authentic,

two theologians met for lunch, self-aware, detached. We've grafted any
    number of theories

over the ahistorical interpretations branded on us in our youth, word-
    woven and layered

the way the untheological talk around us is plaited into the restaurant's
    comforting noise,

stoneware striking stoneware, rattle of ice, laughter as coarse as a surform
    tool

shaping hardwood stock in a vice. We add some noise of our own:
    Unamuno

and Messiaen, presence in absence, sketch study, line readings, our
    choice

of three vegetables jotted down by the waitress who calls us *hon'*. The
    braying

air-conditioner in the wall is as calming as half-awake liturgy. When
    you're this hungry

it's not even slumming. "That which is only living," Eliot wrote
    somewhere

in the *Quartets*, "can only die." We look around this dinful room and tell
    ourselves

we know the difference. The books we have read assure us it's the books
    we have read

that will save us. Ketchup on the chicken livers—call it comfort food, soul
    food. Yeah,

I'll have the pie. Neither of us would say it aloud, but maybe the world is a
   heap

of miracles, one on top of another. The table of plumbers laughs as one, a
   laughter

they attempt to fend off but fail. If miracles are to mean anything at all,
   they'll mean it

here, where they might raise an eyebrow. What's not miraculous about
   meringue half a foot tall,

airy and sweet? We only order it to have an excuse to drink another cup of
   coffee, a reason to kill

another few minutes while the last of the noon crowd clears out of the
   restaurant, making it

more like the rooms we absented, which are silent and will stay that way even
   when we return

to switch on the desk lamp, our work right where we left it, laid out so
   carefully, but still just words

darkening a page. I'll have to look at them a long time before they turn again
   to sounds on my ear.

Arkansas Stone

It's the dull blade that will cut you, I was always told.
My grandfather's whetstone was worn to a concave arc,
a beautiful line more fitting to describe the first ripple
in a stone-pierced pond, or the wind-bent contrail
drawn by a jetliner too high to leave its sound,
than to be a shape eroded into a hand-sized piece of rock.
The hone felt cool and soft, too soft for its work,
it seemed to me. And when he let me sit beside him
on the porch steps towards the end of a Saturday visit
to try my hand at putting an edge on the sheep's clip
of an old three-bladed Boker, the afternoon's light
untangling from the uppermost limbs of the black gum tree,
I was disappointed at how little effect each stroke had.
My grandfather had already learned the uses of patience,
how these lives we're given are made mostly of waiting
and incremental wear and a life's work of standing up
against it. In the day's deliberate ending, he worked the blade
too quickly to see but with no sense of haste, the steel
licking at the oiled stone of a bottomless, hopeless thirst.
My grandfather loved his pocketknives. At any time
he might have about his person a Schrade Old Timer
or a lock-blade Buck, a treebrand Boker or any
of an assortment of Double-X Case knives which I knew
to be his favorites, the Case brand oval countersunk
into the bone handle, all of them dressy knives the size
of a ring finger or less, something a man might carry
in his suit pants pocket on the way to worship.

He traded them during smoking breaks on the loading dock
at the Salant & Salant shirt factory, each one with a story
of its complicated provenance—what exchanged, how much
to boot. Even the ones he had paid too dearly for made a tale
just as willingly told, words as fine as the blade edge
he would keep on the knife, able to cut straight
to what was intended and nowhere else, easily
and without error. I now know he loved the stories
more than the objects that occasioned them. I never questioned
the reasoning or the desire behind collecting such things,
and still don't. Who would ever say a knife
is not a piece of art, so precisely made and perfectly
folded, so blissfully singular of purpose? We would love
to know our place in the world and snap into it
with such finality, kept true with a drop of 3-In-One oil.
Isn't all beauty just this dangerous? I am tempted to say
that the contemplation of every beautiful thing can tear us
free from this life, opening us in all the ways
a knife wound may: a deep puncture that seals itself and aches,
or any number of gashes and tears and cuts that bleed sullenly
and won't properly close, troubling us as they heal and even
after they do. We talk about beauty in the same words. We say
it cuts us to the quick. We say it pierces us, and it does.
Last year I bought an Arkansas stone for myself, higher quality
than my knives need or I deserve, a piece of novaculite quarried
near Hot Springs. The rock is cream-colored, grayed
at the ends already from the ground-in fine leavings
of steel blades brought impatiently down its length
time and time again. I fear I am forgetting everything

I have been taught. Most of the time I can't even feel
the changes the world is forcing me to, where the day bears on me
and where I press back. Why not put it this way: I am being honed
like a brittle blade; my heart is a length of carbon steel
folded into a bone handle, blackened and pitted
from my own poor care; it shines only where it has been hit
by the whetstone, the loosely bound atoms aligned
against the randomness of their will, the way the world
wears us down to what we are, every day another layer
ground away, too little to see, and you hope the world's strokes
are directed toward some comprehensible purpose, simple as stone
on tempered steel, taking you to a finer point, an edge
that shines in the right light and is sharp enough to not cut.

Burning the Walls

I took the torch to work today, the site
on Circle Street, that tall frame house you dreamed
we'd someday live in. Remember the Sundays we drove
through neighborhoods finding dream homes?
We don't do it anymore. We hardly get up
from the kitchen table and never speak of
the thirty-year note or moving from this shadeless street.
I paint the houses we looked at and could tell you
about their insides. You say I don't make enough
for my effort. Does anyone? But this is work
I understand. I can follow the repetition
of long brush strokes, the governed paths of the roller.
Everything I know is just motions now
and the getting through them, how you say goodbye the same
each morning, leaning to not touch
my painter's whites that hide a million spatters,
how my hand always finds the same place
on your shoulder, the other hand
the same place on the enameled door frame.
The house on Circle Street had to be burned.
Have I ever told you why that is done?
Paint builds up. Twenty years of exterior oil base,
every new coat a little less even
until it has to be burned from the siding, and you start over.
If it's done right it is all new.
You would be amazed. I've taken off paint and found wood
still green. I swear to God sometimes

you can see the pencil marks
left by the carpenter's helper, the black stamp
of the Weyerhaeuser tree. The nailheads
will be gray and shiny. You can count the circles
each place the nail was driven too far
and the hammerhead struck.
You say we never talk and you know nothing
about what I do or how I feel about it.
I will tell you this. I spent all day
on an aluminum ladder. My hands are shaking
from holding the propane torch and keeping the flame
the right distance away. The paint doesn't blaze
at once. It wrinkles like apples on the ground
and slowly a bubble comes up, the first oxygen
getting beneath the paint. Then it burns.

Philosophy

I can't say the car was broken into since I'd forgotten to lock it. When I
    went out

to get the paper, the day quarter-lit and unbegun, the trunk was thrown
    open,

its bulb lamp a weak addition to what the sunrise had a mind to get
    going.

I stood there in the new light, and then I began the inventory. Jumper
    cables

and a field chair gone, a faucet set I'd been meaning to return to the
    home center,

some hurricane relief donations we hadn't gotten around to dropping
    off

at Catholic Charities—bottles of shampoo, multipacks of soap and
    toothbrushes,

assorted store brand cleansers. The disposable diapers, baled into dense
    packages,

were still there. But not my Johnny Cash CDs or the digital voice
    recorder

left in the console with some teaching notes and the beginnings of a
    grocery list

spoken into its memory, and a single image: *unginned cotton woven in the
    road weeds.*

Or something like that, a few muttered words that sounded better
    before they'd been

stolen from me. When a thief took his lamp, Epictetus cursed himself
    for owning one

worth coveting. It takes a week of working at it before I can apply
    philosophy

to even the smallest loss, atom-thin as the coatings on a pair of
    binoculars' prisms,

a trick to let in the light more perfectly. Here's what I'll say: It's just urban life.

Crimes of opportunity. We live with them, like traffic and mosquitoes. I'll say

it's the cost of doing business in the old part of town—every now and then you have to

throw a lawn mower into the volcano. A philosopher's consolations, these weary tenets

of dead men's systems, knocked together so I might stop thinking how somewhere

some thieving bastard is listening to Johnny and June trade verses on *Live at Folsom Prison*.

Anagnorisis

In the coffee shop everyone is reading or talking, and the music murmurs a kind
    of commentary

we want to believe has something to say about us, even as entire phrases get
    obliterated

by our peals of serrate laughter and the espresso machine's roar. I can still piece
    together

"Dear Old Stockholm," and then "In Walked Bud" and "She Rote." I'm supposed
    to say

the world's a midden of word shards and failed gesture, a steaming pile of
    misprision, all noise

and chance. We never connect. I've read the Language poets and the new novel.
    It's a secret

that keeps getting found out and never fails to make us feel wised up: we don't say
    what we mean

and couldn't if we wanted to, our words betray us at every turn, no one listens
    and no one hears.

Week before last, the baristas were playing country music. Hank on that lost
    highway, Ernest Tubb

waltzing across Texas, Delta Dawn what's that flower you have on? Like Ray
    Charles said,

it's the stories. Just a note or two and I could rebuild the whole song—verse,
    bridge, chorus.

What we do is collect and assemble, dosed up with caffeine and whatever else
    might nerve us

to shape the world into something orderly and tellable. It's all artifice. Even
    sitting here

minding my own business. Silence is rhetoric, the purest exposition. At a two-top
    against the wall,

a man is reading a Greek play in a Penguin Classics edition. Everyone here
    believes

anagnorisis is not just a strategy for the stage but what we all are due: a moment
of recognition,

sudden and searing. It's coming soon, our own crisis and unraveling. Here in this
room

full of people making stories, every posture and pose is a mode of development.
Sitting alone

reading back issues of *Mother Jones* or a used paperback of *Compañero: The Life and
Death*

of Che Guevara is a kind of declamation, a heartbreaking story told in the way a
tattoo's blue smear, bared

at the shoulder next to the pinkish sateen of a bra strap, is made muddied by the
skin imprisoning

the ink, a yin and yang disk that one evening not long ago may have seemed to
explain something

about this admixture of hope and sure death we somehow savor. In a worn-out
wingback,

she drinks her *au lait* with a Camus-like courage, a Sartrean disdain, and there is
much

to be read in the way the page gets turned. We come here to sit over coffee and tell
our own version

of how nothing means and nothing follows. I've noticed we're getting better at it,
each day

another iteration, a revision of the story more coherent and seamlessly said with
each bitter sip.

At Marx's Grave

The guidebook said it wouldn't be easy to find. I was killing an hour
in London, a student on holiday, my first time abroad. I remember
the sun could almost make a shadow. The path took a turn and then
there was Marx's marble head, looming, unconcerned at the shabbiness
of his surroundings. How could I miss it? The new section of Highgate
looked old enough to me, the weeds a brutal green, seeming to press
the markers up out of the sod and throw them over until they were broken
into pieces the earth could swallow. Not a single plumb stone
in the place. This is what death is: weeds and confusion, the end
of tidiness. Even the silence will be shriven of its elegance and converted
into something it wasn't before, just another of the infinite variations
on noise. All I could say I had in common with Marx was a fondness
for writing in libraries. And maybe the same starting point: it is here
that we hurt, in this world built of dust and lies—our bruises
the best knowledge we get. If nature is never spent, as Hopkins would have it,
surely it is to drive home the lessons we resist. My neck was stiff from sleeping
on the floor of a nurses' dormitory near Victoria Station, the rooms so cold
the girls used the window sills to keep their milk and butter and jam cool
all week long. My soul won't come loose from the conditions that encompass it,
these shadow-casting facts I lean on; it pushes against them, just as I tested
the blistering cold granite of the monument, wondering why everything must seem
immutable. If the weeds would give up an answer, I wouldn't need to struggle
to write down the yieldings and accommodations I arrive at. Sometimes I believe
the greatest truth is the feel of a legal pad under the pencil's point, the hiss
as my hand slides from word to word across a page which only appears to be
free of texture, trying to gather what sounds might make the day
keep remembered. My mother's second husband gave her a gravestone bigger

than Marx's head. You can see the thing a mile down the highway, pointing
the surest way out of the earth. It has her life story carved in it and her likeness sealed
like a cameo under glass. This was not something she asked for. Birds perch
on the stone's apex for the prospect it gives over the narrow section
of highway, the fields and the uncut timber edging them. Where I come from
the sun can get so bright even the shadows seem to shine. How long
might a stone like that last before the earth takes it back? That day
in London I took a snapshot and got back on the Underground. Sometime later
I put down a few impressions in my notebook, probably on the all-night ferry
from Newhaven to Dieppe, or on the train down to Paris, certainly after dark
when there was little to see except my own face reflected in the dulled glass
of the passenger compartment. The new acid-free papers are guaranteed
to remain stable for over four hundred years, but no part of me will live on
in these words I'm arranging. I would like to say I'm here, on this page, and always
will be, but I'm not. I'm well behind the marks I've made on draft after draft, cut off
from what they almost said, beyond the simple oppositions of this place, soon to be
about such repose as may be had in the cool and weedy ground, a good place to lie
undisturbed and still, the white stone at my head settling out of plumb, a poem folded
in my breast pocket, another piece of this world that won't cross with me to the next.

Book Loaned to Tom Andrews

I'd already found out that one of the secrets to happiness was never loan your
    books. But I loaned it anyway. We were all of us poor and living

on ideas, stumbling home late to basement apartments, talking to ourselves.
    What did we own except books and debt? When the time came

we could move it all in the trunk of a car. Tom knew what a book was worth—he
    brought it back a week later, seemingly unhandled, just a little looser

in the spine, a trade paper edition of *The Death of Artemio Cruz*, required reading
    for a course in postmodernism we were suffering through.

The book's trashed now, boxed up and buried in the garage with a hundred other
    things I can't throw away. When I moved back south I loaned it again

to a girl I'd just met. At some party I'd said it was the best novel since *Absalom,*
    Absalom!, which may have been true, but mostly I was trying to impress her,

and convince myself, still testing all I'd been told about how the matter of a book
    is best kept separate from, well, matter. Months later, it turned up

on my front steps without comment, the cover torn in two places, the dog-eared
    pages of self-conscious prose stuck together with dark, rich chocolate.

Rest

After the commute I try not to think about it. I close the car door
and the concussion fills the garage, an endsound, the final dying note
of some inscrutable and dissonant piece, then just the ticking of an engine
losing its heat to the temperate evening. The backyard is strewn
with toys lying on their sides, wheels in the air, all abandoned to let fall
where they may, the fruitless efforts to get our child to put things up
when he's done with them. Only the tools does he take seriously enough
to put in their place, the toy shovel and hoe and rake leaned in a neat row
against the potting bench. An hour and fifteen minutes on the road
and I haven't even loosened my tie. All I remember is highway disappearing,
always more of it waiting behind the next low hill, the patience of everything
with no end in sight. I have learned I can look at the road hard enough to forget
I ever passed over it. The blinds of the house are golded with light. The oak tree
looms above the steeply pitched roof just where I left it, but now daubed
with the gold rebeginnings of leaves, claiming a little more of the sky
than when I last looked. I want to leave the day behind and be no place
but here. You know how hard it is. The black paint of the car is yellowed
with as much of this year's pollen as would hold on against the wind
of the interstate. Is there no pure thing, nothing without story
clinging to it, undusted by our speculations and judgment, cut loose
from its past and so simplified it has meaning before we give it meaning?
There is but a short interval left to the day, little time to recover, and I want
to slow it to a standstill. Little enough that can be thought of as rest, everything longs
to keep going. I usually hesitate on the concrete drive, just for a half beat,
the promise of home almost too sweet to take a breath of. I look down
at the cracked sections of the driveway and try to get the cords of my neck

to loosen. When I was a boy my father stood me before a mirror in the bedroom
and taught me to tie a tie, a Windsor and a half-Windsor knot, and the four-in-hand
I still use. He also told me the silk must rest. In a minute, I will take off my tie
and drape it over a black peg in the tie rack screwed to the inside of the closet door,
a place of quiet and repose where the sheeny fabric will try to find a way
to forget its dimple and crease, the bend and cinch of the long day's knotting.

Daylight

God is proven in some way by the extreme difficulty of believing in him...
—SIMONE WEIL

July already, and the land is soon to burn, the sun at midday casting
its least shadow. Across the road, the unmown pasture will whiten
under its glare, and the world goes brittle with heat.
The land loves the light, and suffers from the light, and lets it go
when the day is done. The illuminated air has a density, and I feel
as though I should part it with my hands when I step from the shade.
You don't have to look hard to see that the light is always leaving—
even rising towards you, taking its lowest angle down the countryside,
it is passing. The days should be getting shorter but I can't sense it
in the slow coursing of this one. It is difficult to believe
even the things you've seen; there is nothing that I know
for certain. A mockingbird lands on a post and has more to say
about what will bear us skyward than I do. The day is without music—
or any that is organized in a way I can hear. It is easy to forget
the words you've read in books and all you've been told is true
with the world this bright and close at hand. I am learning to look
with a new kind of wanting. There are a few minutes as the day dims
when the details in the distant line of trees become clarified,
the tree forms taking on greater depth, their lobed leaves individuated
as the light releases them, the rich texturing of each tree
suddenly present, rendered with a painstaking draftsmanship,
then they blacken and solidify, emptied of every last particular,
a jagged line backed by a sky which will stay brilliant for some time
to come, as though the light that once lay in the weeds now waits
in the air above, wondering, I suppose, why it is we do not follow.

How I'm Telling It

Even the burns on her arms were a poem to me. I'm ashamed to
   say

that's what I remember, more than the flatness of her voice, more
   than

the uncertain quality of the brown in her eyes. When I think
   about it,

I should not have been let loose with the language. The words
   were so new

to me then: they rose and sighed at my touch, and pain was just
   another excuse

to hear what the world would sound like in my own broken voice.

She had a job in a bakery, and I remember her colorless skin
   festooned

with the angry markings of her mistakes, the slightest
   ungoverned motion

as she reached into the dark of the oven, the white flesh on the
   underside of her wrist,

where the skin is smoothest, almost translucent, now marred by
   an instant's touch

with the rolled lip of a loaf pan. The work was done in the black of
   morning, half-awake,

when she was half-thinking about the shapes of her own poems.
   That's how I'm telling it

now, the memory or two I have to work from pressed flat and
   dried by the years.

I knew her, it's true, but not enough to ask her what the world was
   doing to us

and how she felt about it. So I am taking that away from her here,
   all that was inside of her,

her voice, the timbre of her thinking, what we may as well call her soul.
   I can tell you

we all worked somewhere, some low-paying job we were glad to get, a
   five-finger exercise

of our lives to come, the lives we said we didn't want, the going to work
   and paying

our own way. We would leave art behind if we could, our notebooks
   and draft pages

packed in the bottom of a box salvaged from a liquor store incinerator.
   Maybe it was all

for the best. I used to believe any poem would ennoble writer and
   reader alike.

What harm could a poem do? I recited them like lines of a catechism.
   But listen to me

wring her humanity from her: she is a glance, a memory I make pretty,
   her pain

something I will decorate with a word like *translucent* or *festoon*. Can it
   be

I still haven't learned the mark a word can make? Forgive me, Father.
   How does it sound

if I say the words touch us and we are burned? Does it sound at all

like what happens? I still can't quite believe many of the things I know,
   the cost

of the slightest overreaching, no matter how quick we are to pull back,
   the only words

worth using reddened and blistering with our waste passions and
   hoarded fears.

The job probably wasn't that bad. The bakery was a popular place with
   our crowd. I imagine her

coming out of the back, flour on her face, tired from her shift but
   pleased to find some friend,

sitting down in the cool morning air at one of the metal tables on the
sidewalk

so in demand back then, the smells of yeast and the oven's heat following
her

even outside, a clinging fiercer than memory. If we could sit down today
over coffee

and something sweet, I would tell her to look at the mark on the back of my
hand

where a drunken woman with a cigarette left a burn on me at a house party
twenty years ago

in Dyersburg, Tennessee. I remember it happening. I was standing in the
kitchen, talking

to one of the two people there that I knew, raising my voice to be heard over
the music

and meaningless laughter if I had anything to add. I turned and saw her
arm's slow arcing—

I will say I could even smell the menthol of the cigarette smoked down to its
filter,

and for some reason the unfolding of the event arrested my attention and
all I could do was watch

until I felt it burn. The scar is so old now it hardly shows; sometimes I can't
even find it,

but when the light settles against my hand at a certain slant, like this, the
closed wound shines.

Accompaniment

Clara Dishman taught the piano lessons in my hometown. Every Tuesday,

Schaum's blue *Piano Course B* under my arm, I rode my bike up Church Street

and leaned it against the white clapboards of the house she'd cut into a duplex

after her husband died. This was what she did to get by, rent to young marrieds

from the Cumberland Presbyterian college and teach the notes of the staff

to the disinclined, quarter note and whole rest, this one's Middle C, hands here

at home position. She was so old the town had stopped telling the story

of how she'd gone away to Cincinnati as a young woman to study to be

an accompanist for silent movies, learning to improvise at the keyboard

many-noted figures for the heightening of suspense, stock phrases to punctuate

the weather or comment on the screen's outsized gestures, a handful of notes

in the lower register that might help the night scene, shot one cloudy afternoon,

seem like night. Half a century later, she was still a Reds fan. "That Joe Morgan

went four-for-four in Pittsburgh Sunday night," she would say as I sat down

to play my scales, the sports page of the Memphis paper wrinkled on the tea table

next to her reading chair, the runic print of the box scores hard for her to
    see

even after the cataracts surgery, her eyes a blue as frangible and pallid as
    old china

behind the thick lenses of her glasses. But she didn't have to see the
    music

to know what keys might soon need be struck. Each next note was a
    choice,

but one drawn from a thin quiver of possibilities. I had already begun to
    pretend

I was somewhere else even though the murmuring little town was full of
    things

I would never learn to neatly leave, the Mylar-wrapped spines at the
    public library,

the sponsors painted on the plywood panels of the Little League park's
    outfield fence.

Nothing ever seemed to happen, and the only music I understood was
    the low pull

of the evening freight train laboring on the upgrade out of town. Miss
    Clara's hands

were knobbed and gnarled, a ghost's hands, bent that way by what the
    music demanded,

the purple flawing of the veins across their tendony backs as delicate as
    the figuring

in the marble slabs of the fireplace surround. They kept their own
    knowledge,

a cache of bone-held memory rehearsed in each legatoed phrase. If I had
    played

some small piece passably well despite my indifferent practicing, I would
    ask her,

"Miss Clara, play a sunrise," and she might indulge me with a few
    flourishes

from the old upright, her hands spidering over arpeggios as delicately framed

and breathless as the first light coming unraveled from the treetops. "Go home,"

she would tell me, "and get to work." I should have practiced harder, and most days

I can't call to mind the truths I've been taught, how a little music makes what's lost

real again, transposed from flickering memory to a few short scenes that won't go dim.

In Season

I ran into him yesterday, a poet I once knew, picking over the pyramids of
    fruit

in the produce section, handling each piece with the same slow
    consideration

he may have once reserved for etching his lines into the page. It had been
    years

since I had seen him. In the old days he was a fixture at the poetry
    readings

and in the used bookstores, declaiming some extreme position in the back
    booths

of the Midtown beer joints. Now here we were in the supermarket's
    recirculated air,

respectable and happy to be out of the house for a few minutes, the
    produce all around us

waxed and glossy, in season or not, stacked with such precariousness that
    all our reachings

brought down more than we intended. Such a strange place to be seeing
    him, a cold room

foundering in cold light, unconnected to the past—not the way I would
    have written it.

He told me he wasn't writing anymore: "The older you get the less you have

to say." The world was no longer a place of mystery and voices for him, I
    could tell.

The avocados were just so many chances for guacamole; they weren't
    weighted

with anything other than their own green heft, charged with no greater
    purpose

than their likelihood of casting a shadow. They could explain nothing.
    And to him,

I was just an old acquaintance, an association like a piece of road outside a
     town he left

when he was young, or maybe the faint smell of newly laid carpeting, some
     vague thing

that could drag him backward, a reminder of the years when he stayed out
     to all hours

lighting one cigarette from the burning butt-end of the last, tamping it on
     the table first

to count off a necessary rhythm, as though the innumerable parts in the
     works of the world

moved in some discoverable time signature. He would return to his rooms
     half-drunk,

the other half confounded, and feverishly read poem after poem, in his
     hand a pencil

pitted with tooth marks, writing his own answers in the margins next to
     some poet's

maddeningly trim lines—Merwin's or Creeley's, maybe—driven and
     distracted

by the noise of the night-filled city and how much of it could be brought
     home

to a bright and empty page yellowed with the glow from a single goose-
     necked lamp,

and how he still held on to enough anger at the end of the day to heat a few
     words

so they might rise a little. All in all he seemed much happier, better groomed

certainly, done with looking to lines of poetry as though they could be
     followed

as surely as lines of reasoning, done with seeking some comprehensible
     story

to explain why the night climbs onto us the way it does out of the ditches
     and tree roots

knotted into the loess soil, grabbing hold of everything that had once stood up

in the daylight to throw its sharpened shadow into the street. Maybe I've come

to the same conclusions. I used to write with a fierceness, handling each word

as though it were a hammer and the world a sheet of unstruck bronze, my job to raise it

into some kind of meaningful relief. These years of laboring over draft pages, their edges

curled from much handling and indecision then laid to rest in unlabeled file folders,

and I'm still not sure I shape a damn thing, the concussions of the hammer more noise

than ringing. Most of what I wanted to say lies obscured within the paper's merciless white,

unwilling to tear itself free. When I got home, I put the green avocado on the window sill

where it will wait through the greater part of the week as it ages and softens

all the way down to its solid pit, readying itself to be cut open, its dense meat coming free

of the skin that has protected it until this late moment. My wife will take a fork,

as I've seen her do before, and mash the fruit in a shallow bowl until it creams

and smoothes, mixing in lemon juice and garlic and a dash of salt, the flavors becoming

something other than themselves, a complicated taste made of noonday sun and southerly wind

soughing in the trees, the bitterness of groundwater and a sharp bite like the slow decaying

of wet bark, all colored with the simple sweetness of a flowering that has
 come and gone

at the start of the season, the subtle record of a hundred days of skies clouded
 and clear,

so rich on the tongue that a lifetime won't be long enough to learn how to say
 it.

Poet's Model

Most of the time he doesn't even look at me, his attentions reserved
for the season's blunted smell on the air, or the clouds changing their color
in the hard evening sun, combing his recollection for some shadow detail
in a painting by Vermeer, making a study of the light, the dusty, careworn light—
all things I would call secondary. He closes his eyes as though he is listening
for something. It doesn't even matter if I'm in the room. We hardly fit, anyway,
this butler's pantry where he works so close and airless, our knees touching
then not touching. I sometimes think it is like the beginnings of love,
but only the beginning, the awkward, improbable first glance. Really,
we're not close. Not in that way. Occasionally I'll hear him
sighing "hold still, hold still," like some left-hand accompaniment
too simple even to require thought, and I'll go back to my reading and wonder
how long he's been making those same two words. I tell myself,
the compensation is in the incidentals, buried in whatever fleeting sense
of importance may come from being the center of attention, the object
under consideration. How many of us can claim to have inspired something
out of nothing, to have pulled blue ink from the tired and empty air?
I know what he'll say better than he does, I know the words
he would like to use but can't put his hands on, I know the words he keeps
in his pocket but lacks the nerve to let be heard. He tries to think of them
as things other than they are: joists and studs maybe, lumberyard pine shot through
with tenpenny nails. I know what the words will bear and what they'll let loose.
I am, after all, what he's trying to nail down. He keeps me on
because I'm discreet. If you're going to go into this line of work, you'd better do it
out of love. The hours are long and tedious. When he puts his hands on me
it's just to remind himself that I'm real, that there's a starting place
to the shadows I cast. Hold still, hold still. I can't tell if he's saying it

to me or to the diamonded lightshapes elongating on the floor.
He looks down and sees an eyelash on the page—his or mine,
what difference? I know him: he will say it's mine, a part of me
lost, now sheltered in this house of words he has spent the day framing.

While the River Is Wide

It is helpful to be reminded how the sun sets
unfailingly fast and final no matter the clearness or the depth
of haze, reddening and trailed out
like a turning wake in placid water. I believe
we should make these steps away from each other
as difficult as possible, as wary and tentative
as our coming together, hoping
they will matter more this way; but we will take them, regardless,
by the end of the summer. I am wearing a ring
and doing what I should have done
from the beginning, marrying a man it took time
to convince, and then troubling to explain my compulsion.
But whoever hears these thoughts? I used to consider them
hurtful voices inside my head which need be heavily shielded.
I've learned, since, that they are incidental
as the sirens passing along Union Avenue, hardly heard
and quickly silenced: they leave us
untouched, their dangerous irradiation lost
in the decay of our reconsiderings.
I am on the highest piece of bluff, and the unsteadiest.
A railroad line once ran its crest but was lost
when a section collapsed in a dry summer,
the drop in the water table loosening a lens
of sand left undetected by the guessing geology
employed back then. There is a steam locomotive buried
below Riverside Drive, a machine so large,
built onto tracks, I suppose, that it wasn't feasible to raise it

once it had fallen with the bluff. Maybe no one knew
a way. So they covered it with earth, invisible, to become story.
I have been down here at night, on this vantage point
when the bridge lights laid their curves
onto the water that appeared, to my eyes,
almost to be standing in place. But this evening,
in the remaining daylight, I can see worshipfully
each wave's edge and progress, the defined unrest of the boiling river
as my thinking roils from me and over its own horizon.
I had wanted to think about someone
I knew who would with faith write down these thoughts
in my head if he could. He would love
to know I am pondering rivers, how as they age
they become more tortuous in their route downward, to whatever sea
is awaiting them and their finally powerful
unloading. He would remark how a great river can change course
in its rushing search for the lowest, most amenable path
and leave a bent leg of water in its straightening,
an oxbow lake miles long that will stay for a time,
and gradually go dry and overgrow, leaving a sandy stain
of the river's passage. He would like this.
But I am concerned with the view from here
and little else, only looking westward
towards where I will move and live at the end
of the summer, leaving this river to its narrowing, leaving
the days to smolder and ready, the next season
rumored in the cooling and spread of these shadows, already
the sun setting every night further downstream.

Prooftext

When I couldn't stand it anymore, I would turn on the television, anything

to get some sound in the house. Sunday morning programming, a show

called *Search the Scriptures* on a station out of Paducah, Kentucky. No matter

what you've heard, there is little to call peaceful about these small towns.

Slowness is not peace. I would walk through the rooms I rented and listen

to the unhurried murmurs the town made, constant and rhythmic, as subtly troubled

as the nighttime respirings of a light sleeper. There was never silence. I could hear

the callings of town birds and the first church-bound cars on North Highland sounding

more like a river than a procession of machines, the shirr of tires seeming to linger

even after their passing, and from somewhere close by, the unending phrase

of a window unit air-conditioner, running more for its comforting drone, surely,

than to bring about any cooling in the spent dawn's mildness—all of it coming

to me through the screen door as though summoned, or needed somehow. Soon

the girl in the apartment next door would begin to play the eight dejected notes

of her scales, then again, a whole tone higher, the hammers like rainfall striking

the spinet's brittle wires, an ascension and descent the walls of the
building couldn't hold.

It was the last place I lived alone. On the television, a man in a poorly
fitted suit

was reading the letters of dispirited viewers, all questions, religious or
not, answerable

by a single verse of the Bible, or more likely a piece of a verse,
something

from the minor prophets or the Acts of the Apostles or the Revelation
of John, prooftexts

he could stack up like a child's wooden blocks worn and rounded at
the edges

from so much handling, softwood grain showing through saliva-
thinned paint.

He held up the folded sheaves of a letter for the camera as though to
prove

there was a letter, an uncompelling visual. But I wasn't watching.
Those days

I would have said a ream of typing paper still in its wrapping had more
proof in it

than all the prooftexts in a proselyte's well-thumbed Scofield Bible.
Nothing

is easy to read. In those days I would have said the only thing a text
can prove

is that the page was probably better off before the words landed
there.

The TV preacher must have expended some effort to forget the
absence

behind the rise of every sound. The world is simple only for those with
no belief.

Without the intrusions of context our lives are almost comprehensible,
so much easier

to say I love you, without having to say I love you here, in this place, amongst

this noise, the bickering of the birds, the distant door slams, what sounds like

a hesitantly picked out Bach invention, hands separate then together, resounding

to an empty room, a black-and-white television playing unwatched on a kitchen counter.

If God has anything to say about it, the words will enter through the door's screen, borne in

on the morning air, a rich assault of sounds which pass and don't pass, which end

and fail to end, diminishing then returning with the day's steady resumption, like the light

just now beginning to collect on the grass in misshapen pieces cut by the new leaves,

the same light that yesterday could find no means to cleanly and simply depart.

New Bill Meyer Stadium

home of the Knoxville Blue Jays

Do you remember the rain delay, anything
that was said? Directly behind home plate,
we had seen the break of every curveball,
the catcher leaning outside with a target
low and away. I believe you asked, does it count
for anything? This is the minor leagues
and nobody remembers who wins or finishes
in the cellar. Here, everyone is waiting
to be called up, waiting whole seasons.
And only the scouts remember
the catches and not even the actual catches
at that, just the potential the catch implies,
the range, how good the hands,
the eye, the strength of an arm.
But every at bat is a drama. There is still
a fence out there. Did I make it clear
how easy it is to forget
the humbleness of the venue with a play on
and runners to protect, behind in the count?
Under the overhang, we watched the night rain
pool and glare in the blue wrinkles
of the infield tarp. We waited it out, largely silent
in the emptying stands, until the grounds crew
began work, confident this long letup
would be for good, and the umpires

conferred on the mound.
Retaking the field, the promising
nineteen-year-old center fielder out of Tempe, Arizona
looked over his shoulder at the spray of spring rain
his polished spikes gleaned from the grass.

Gray

The mornings drag on, arriving at a quality of grayness impossible
at a more complicated hour. I am used to the rooms of the house
being empty, their quiet as fast to me as the bone-colored paint
against the plaster, a slate slow to take the color of day. I find a note
beside the telephone, your blueprint script, all caps and perfectly aligned,
the chisel point characters deep in the paper from your pressing, almost silver
on the bleached page. Our lives are filled with language and its exchange—
pieces of barter to buy off the silence leaving its tinge over everything
like vegetable ink rubbed from the newsprint of the morning paper.
What we can't say is still language. These shadowy emotions are words
even when we don't know the words. We succeed in telling a small part only,
a detail of the picture, but it's worth the writing down, if only one word
is partway true. Put it in a note left in the topmost drawer; chances are
it will be discovered. The writer of the book of James believes life is no more
than a breath of air, invisible and fluid, a vapor soon dispersed. I know the winds
may only be traced by what they manage to pick up and carry, scraps of paper
written over with fading characters, left behind to be found and read again.

Paper Anniversary

A forgiving spring and now July's heat. You can almost see
the grass growing. In the mornings, white-throated sparrows take turns
flying through the spray of lawn sprinklers up and down
the street. Our driveway bends around an ancient pin oak—you tell me
it is a willow oak, *Quercus phellos*, but I will keep calling it
what I have always heard it called. This is how names work:
they come about somehow and stay if they stay. We are still
unpacking, finding resting places for the belongings we brought
to this old house, the silverware and wedding china, odd pieces
of furniture, cartons of papers and books, the heaviest things
to move. It has been the season of discovering the yard's plantings,
blooming in their time to speak what we'll take as a welcome. The azaleas
announced themselves to us as pink or white, solving that mystery
before coloring the lawn with discarded flowers. You were happy for a week
when you discovered the peonies languishing and neglected
beside the one good section of fence on the property and could hardly wait
until their lavish blooms shamelessly came open. The hydrangeas, you say,
have their color decided for them by the soil's subtle chemistry.
You brought in panicles of blossoms mostly the tint of a day-sky's blue
in a cooler season, but also shaded with tincture of iodine and a wash of rust
to complicate the hue. All of this is news to me. Every flower
has at least two names. Butterfly bush, summer lilac, something in Latin
I would have to look up. Since we moved in, you have been arranging
cut flowers from the yard in what vases we have, the widemouth jar
I found in the crawl space, a beaded white stem vase handed down
from somebody's grandmother, the blue bottle vase I paid a few dollars for
at a secondhand shop, purple iris against the parchment-colored walls, a spray

of narcissus on the dresser. Le Corbusier said, "The plan proceeds from within
to without; the exterior is the result of an interior." Outside, on this narrow city lot
a sense of order arises as I take up the chain saw and clear away a decade's worth
of mimosa volunteers and wild cherry trees. I can see the plan that someone laid out
before us, hollies in a line below the dining room window, the bulbs arrayed
around the house's corner and in a long bed beside the garage, a declivity in the lawn
where a flowering tree must have stood. In early summer a single surprise lily
emerged two feet tall overnight with a trumpet flower. We will make our revisions.
I prune the ivy and pull it from where it has climbed the window screens.
The massive oak, seventy years old, planted the year the house went up,
has endured as long as anything on this street. We should stop worrying
what to call things. Something will come to us, a phrase that holds
a like meaning for you as it does for me. I've found the place where the soul goes
when it is set loose from the body. I do not know the word for it.

Ornithology

The sky is different here, but even in town we pay attention to the birds,
    judging them

the way we judge everything else eking out a difficult life. I don't envy
    them, such effort

to become airborne, their frighted wings beating against the pavement,
    raising the dust

before they raise themselves. The neighbor's cats take their toll, well
    enough fed

but hunting anyway. They blandly toy with the dying songbirds, wounded
    house wrens

and finches, bloodied and disoriented, blind to the bending of their own
    fate, still hoping

for flight. We all do what we do to keep going without giving it much
    thought.

We would never classify the acts that fill our days as struggle. Anything
    can be a science

save your own life. Who can be detached from that? We look to nature and
    hope to find it

beautiful and transcendent, somehow beyond our lowly doings, but it's
    best not to look

too closely. The birds take flight for a time, and I will aver they are
    beautiful

while it lasts. I sometimes wonder if love is not a thing to be
    accomplished

but what we are, no more a choice than the color of our eyes. Last
    summer

I put off cutting down the mimosa tree because of the robins
    nesting

in its leggy branches. I stood at the window and watched them
    flying

load after load of straw and twigs and mud into the tree, shaping the
    nest

with the curvatures of their own bodies, a furiously constructed
    extension

of their own earthly form. It was a tree ill-suited to home building. In a
    thunderstorm

I watched from the window while one of the birds sat the nest without
    complaint

as the tree swayed wildly in the wind, the weather, to me, merely
    something to enfold

into my writing, a vehicle I might freight with some precious meaning,
    artificial

and delicate, arranged and rearranged in these marked-up draft pages
    dealt out

on the desktop as deliberately as a losing hand of solitaire. I never saw
    them after that;

they must have given up the nest. I found a shard of blue shell on the
    grass, light enough

for flight in the least wind, possessed of a strength of design that is
    sometimes sufficient.

I took the tree down the next day, a piece at a time so it wouldn't
    reach

the power service when it fell, the branches with their prehistoric fronds
    gliding

to the ground below my twelve-foot ladder. Mimosas are beautiful in
    June

but they are more weed than tree, breeding so many volunteers in the
    small city yard

where I intended shortly to teach my own children how to walk. I had no remorse,

the chainsaw ripping at the wet wood, coating my gloved hands and the bare skin of my arms

with sawdust regular and squared, not a form found in nature but the shape of its ruin.

Nocturne

To be heard in this house we must say the words as though cutting them

into polished stone, phrasings hewn to resist what the night will do. Even at this hour

the table lamp's bulb can scribe only a loose circle on the floor, its yellow light

pushing against the corner shadows, the slurred last note of a one-note work song.

Everything has a voice. Words fly from us sharp as marble chips, and a fine dust settles

on the toe moldings and window trim. If we move with enough care we can live here

for years and stir nothing at all. The tops of the picture frames wear a velveteen husk

of dusty apology—a gloved finger would peel up a story I told you one night in August.

The few things I am sure of must be said as quarter notes, an iteration so slow

it will become hard to recall the first faltering word where the sentence began, back

when you were still listening. This city is never quiet. At midnight, every night,

the cargo planes begin their scream and strain, somehow shrugging their way clear

of the black earth. It is hard to tell when the sound of one plane is gone and another

takes its place. God knows where they will set down again. I believe there is no erasing

what is said, even if it goes unheard and unheeded. The words will gather

somewhere. It's hard enough to know what we mean to say, and that
isn't the half

of saying it. To find what is speakable in my heart will take all night. The
best time is just before

the darkness splinters with new light, the dawning ready to be sectioned
by the bent blades

of the venetian blinds, opalescent lightstrands to lift the night's weight
from your skin. It helps

if the words are simple and worth saying. It helps if the first thing I say
is your name.

Prayer

The midmorning sun, low-angled, wedge sharp. My soul longs
to be brimmed full and trued like the shadow line the barn casts
down the snowy pasture, slipping inchmeal into its fate, conformed
to the irregular ground, drawing up toward midday, compact, intensified,
then turning back eastward, straight as a carpenter's chalk line
with its small bursts of blue feathering either side of its demarcation,
fine as the fibers coming unspun from a length of yarn, a looseness
to the line, the complex meeting between sunlight and umbra taking
some small space to work itself out. The shining snow is painful and pointless
to look on with its emptied whiteness, but the snow in shade is otherwise—
gray-blue and seemingly lit from below, black blades of fescue
lanced through at such angles as please them, an artist's crosshatchings,
hand applied, serving to give what is merely surface the effect of depth,
the apprehensibility of the real. The silo's needle-shadow comes in
to compass the floor of this room, the same flat arc a sundial's gnomon
would trace. Every earthly thing is a clock counting down to its coming
unfixed, its perfect dissolution. Whatever I've believed, I know my soul
to be the smallest piece of an infinite wanting, describing an emptiness
in the fiery cloth it was cut from, edge-seared, wordless. Over there, the silhouette
of some low-forking tree, riotous and sharp, engraves the frozen ground.

Winter

This turning inward. It's the season for it: first day of winter and I can
  hear

the brittle limb tips scratching at the bricks whenever the wind stirs
  them. Don't think

that because an emotion gets harder to describe it becomes any less real.
  Our love

is now many roomed, so built-out and sprawling I get lost inside it, and I
  wonder

how did that simpler love sustain us in its one lambent chamber, the
  corners cast

into edgeless shadow? Now our son singing a carol in the chapel is
  enough

to make me reassign the meanings clung to all the words I've ever
  used

to mean love. The inhumed ache of it is what I didn't expect, this
  wintering out,

a splinter under the skin too deep and fine to get at. Last year's storm

uprooted the four oaks shading this lot, and, ever since, we can't help but
  pay attention

to the sound of the wind, its one long word caught in the storm windows,
  as haunting

as a theme from one of those Bartók quartets I've tried to get out of my
  head,

or the half-memory of the road roar from a car trip when I was a
  child

almost asleep on the backseat. Even weather-stripped and dampered

shut, this house can't keep quiet. The strain of the wind load, the press of
  it

borne by the balloon framing, makes the walls speak occasionally, a
  stutter

like the last tic of a run-down timepiece. If I knew what they were trying
to tell me

I would write it here. I am interested in what persists, like the stretch of
silence

bared when the wind lays for a moment, the silence that was always
present, as real

as the ground frozen under a fitful night's dusting of snow. In the
washed last-light,

the trees that still stand have lost their leaves now at year's end, but if
you look

there is a delicacy this evening in how they've opened to admit the pale
sky

into their embrace, doing what they've done in different weather,
reaching

into an emptied heaven to fill it as best they can. Everything that lasts
demands

a new word for itself before long. Words go corrupt and settle and
shift

from the plumb meanings you once nailed them to. Nothing will
stay

without being resaid. When the sun comes up late and cold, our love will
continue

unchanged, only asking of us one unworn word that will say it again,
newly.

The Creative Process

Outside, what's left of a killing frost. Daystart twilight hardens and grays off,

some pale poison drawn from the ground. This is the time of testing

what will survive the winter's regard. Small things, mostly. Easy to miss.

Soybean rust can winter over on the underside of a kudzu leaf. A few ruined buds

persisting on the camellias, skeined so orderly and tight, darkened at the tips—

some years not a one of them will open. The moles haven't stopped prying at

the brick-cold earth, sightless, or close to it, turning according to some felt sign.

The scene that jacks itself up to this high window has been made partial and pared

of detail, filtered through a light only browned a little against the dieback

of Bermuda. The waved panes of glass are whispering something that has a sound

like security, something that sounds like nothing at all. It's so hard to lay hold of

what drifts in the gray winter air, but if it isn't caught up now, worded and rowed,

the frost will turn it to dust, and when the light finally unlimbers, all there was to tell

will have been scoured off in a dry wind, erased by an unsearchable sun always setting,

reclaiming from the colorless bands of winter cirrus the light it only lent us. At the end,

I'll marker it in any desperate way, these half-ordered lines laid down like headstones strewn up a hillside, far back from the road. The day at last drops away, and nothing's left

to say about it. Just a simplification, these final comments and closings, this settling

of past due accounts. At the end, only light scraps and emptiness, palsied street lamps

and a few cold stars gimleted to a dusty sky, just gestures, really, but a kind of writing

after all: scrawled night notes to pick up again if we think of it, to unfold and sound out.

Newground

We would sometimes take the old road home, the unlined asphalt sun-
   brittled
and load-riven, as though our forgetting were just another of the elements
wearing down what's in its way. All summer long the tar had wept out in tiny
   dribs,
blood-black like the ones I imagined on Christ's Gethsemane brow. We were
   in the country,
white pump houses in the side yards of the old homeplaces, briars and scrub
   woods
pitted against the seasonal order of row cropping. We passed a field afire,
   tongues
of flame the size of tongues edging out toward the road's gnawed shoulder.
"Burning off a newground," my father said. I was so young I could hardly
   see
over the dashboard but I knew when he said something just to savor the
   sound of it,
some tired regionalism, a dying word's bended note. What was a newground?
   Something lost,
I supposed, someplace worth lamenting if you had a moment. I was coming
   to suspect
all words had once held a meaning I could only guess at. Most of what I knew
   was just suspicion
I was hoping would solidify to something more dependable. My father didn't
   need to watch
the road much to drive it. We'd rolled the windows down: the smell of a
   place
would linger in the car for a mile or two after we'd put it behind us,
   honeysuckle and cow piles,

the smoke from the field stubble caught up in the heavy air. By the next
time we passed this way

a disc-harrow would have turned the burned-off field, its ashen crust
buried

under coppery new clods of earth carved as smooth as the way you might
remember

a woman's bared shoulder, or the gently curved waves in an old vacation
photograph, neatly rowed

and back-turned against a whitened sky. The ash will wait for the next
crop to leach it

from its dark bed and feed it to the sun, purified. Enough time has passed.
I can tell you now

what a newground is, and I know that *clod* and *cloud* were once the same
word,

but there is a cache of words that were my father's and are not mine to lose
or love,

the way he would toss them out the open car window into the tire whine
and wind roar,

that beautiful road song I'm trying to sing for you, the last miles between
here and home.

Night Air

Toward evening, the air in the house took on the stale taste of safety, and I
    dreaded the time

it all had to change. The rooms spoke in low tones, discernible only at certain
    hours,

but they had stories to tell me if I could find the right ways to listen. After
    dark, one by one

the sashes would be raised, their counterweights falling noisily in the wall's
    hidden hollows,

incandescent light and my mother's voice the only guards against the night
    sounds sifting

through the screens, the murmurs of crickets and the last quarrelsome bird
    cant so distant

and mysterious they might have been the cast off dreams of our neighbors
    retired early

of a late-spring evening. I could smell sleep coming on like the threat of wet
    weather,

and I think I knew even then, when I was a child, that most of the talking
    that got done

was a glossy veneer glued and clamped to a softwood silence. I would have
    done better

to listen to what didn't speak in words: my father's Sunday shirt fallen in a
    white heap

on the bedroom floor, or the kitchen faucet's purposeful dripping into a
    dishcloth draped

over the double sink's divide. Everything the house held had become an
    artifact to foretell

the comings apart we would say we had expected, like painted potsherds
    filtered from the dirt

at an archaeologist's dig. LP records were leaning in the wire racks below a
    record player

I wasn't sure would still work. The album covers had more to say about us than the music,

their cardboard corners blunted and worn, dust sleeves turned to show a black edge of vinyl

poised to be poured out and played, Christmas albums by the likes of Eddie Arnold and Brenda Lee

alongside orchestrated movie themes and show tunes performed by the original Broadway cast,

one warped disk of famous speeches, an inspirational album still in the shrink- wrap.

We were living in fear. I couldn't have put a name to it at the time, but I knew

my parents had chosen for safety. They wanted quiet above all else, too superstitious

to speak a fear aloud or ask for more than was theirs, knowing that to want something

and then to have it would fate us to be destroyed at its loss. For all our fear of excess

and the gods' reprisals, we may as well have been in a play by Aeschylus— the timid chorus

unable to leave the dancing pit, awed watchers talking to ourselves in words that wouldn't slow

the approach of tragedy, our lives a back-and-forth dance in a prescribed place, the center

of a small, delimited world. But what we already had was what we wanted, and each day

was another day of losing it. There were so many things to be afraid of, tornadoes in the night,

rabies and lockjaw, elevator cables snapping and every other kind of metal fatigue,

bank failures and house fires, brown recluse spiders in the cushions of the couch, the Ford

stalling on the tracks at railroad crossings just as a freight train sounds its horn. For all I knew my parents' dreams were filled with such things. They would warn me out of the night air,

my bare feet wet with the accumulating dew, clippings of Bermuda and crabgrass

clinging to my ankles. One of them would call, "Get in here," from behind the screen door

while the moths frayed their pale wings against the fine wire weave which must have appeared

as soft as gray tulle in what light was left. Then, in the voice I heard them use

to pray: "You'll catch your death." And I would wonder exactly when the air switched

from day to night, if something drastic and malevolent happened as the daylight left it,

the onset of the darkness not merely a passive emptying but a crowding out

of all that would sustain us and give us hope by every last thing we had failed

to understand. I remember wanting to ask them what other air would we breathe

when the sun went down? All my studying since then and I still know little about

the nature of darkness and what it contains, but I am beginning to think they were right,

there is something the light takes with it when it goes that changes the cool night air

into an omen. I have my own fears, inherited or accumulated over time, I can't tell you.

I go out for walks at night, anything to get up from this silent typewriter and move

somewhere else, the old foursquares and Italianates looming over the sidewalk as I pass

along Carr Avenue. It is late enough that everyone has turned in for the night, the houses

shut tight and gone dark except for porch lights left on though no one is
    expected, maybe

a reading lamp still burns in an upstairs window. The wet night air is much
    changed

from what the day held, a poorly fitted weight on my skin as heavy as a thrift
    store suit.

I'm afraid my feet will never leave the heaved and broken sections of this
    sidewalk

and the weight of the night's darkness will become more than I can shoulder,
    the sky

with its stars, so few and muted, bowing me down beneath its ill-lit
    nothingness,

and my walking will not end, my head full of the words I will not say aloud,
    for fear.

My Father's Whiskey

It was Baptist whiskey, bought at a package store in the next town or even further
   away and kept hidden

in his sock drawer, a fifth of Old Charter, Bottled in Bond, enough to last him for
   years. A measure or two

might cook the eggnog come Christmas or find its way once in a while into a hot
   toddy to ease a winter cold. When I was younger

I thought it the worst hypocrisy to sock-drawer your satisfactions, I thought it
   wrong to keep anything

inside, really. Opaqueness was corrupt—this was another of the propositions we
   could argue over

for the greater part of an evening. I'm just coming to understand his accounting
   procedures, how he wasn't the poorer

for the silences he kept. My own heart has almost been emptied. If I'd held on to
   my stories a little longer, all those things I said

I would say differently now. It's a slow drip that replenishes the flavors of an
   interior life, the bitter notes blunted

by patient aging in casks of fire-charred oak, the seared staves mellowing the
   liquor's burn because they've been

burnt themselves. Best not to tell it all out, these raw syllables which, like any
   volatile distillate, need long years to grow sweet.

Pastoral

*I find that, as I grow older, I am becoming less susceptible to those feelings of
deepest melancholy that used to come over me when I looked at nature, and I
congratulated myself on this as I walked along.*
—THE JOURNAL OF EUGÈNE DELACROIX

Most of the time I don't even notice the grainy afternoon light cutting across
  these uplands

sharp as a drawknife flaying back the day's veneer, laying it open until there's
  nothing left

to enclave my recollections of all the other days lit just this way. To you,
  everything is simplicity

and sweetness out here in the country—bean fields and hopeful small towns, a
  two-lane highway

climbing a hill, then gone. I have no idea why I ever came back to this latitude. I'll
  be walking

to the post office, happy with the sound of my shoes hitting the sidewalk,
  reprieved from a desk

in a windowless room, and the light out of a mild sky on the thirteenth of May
  will look exactly

the way it's supposed to look, exactly the way the light has looked on every
  thirteenth of May

I've ever known, caught up in the greeny penumbra of the red oaks, laid out
  across the soybeans

rowed in Mr. Brooks's fields, inscribing me. This is what home is, a few shapes on
  the retina

that won't unburn, certain sights sifted out, weightless and finely cut as the sky's
  shiny litter

of cumulus piling higher once the afternoon comes on and heats up. For the most
  part,

landscapes are imagined anyway, chlorophyll and sky tilt, honeysuckle and
  magnolia blossom

loading the wind with a regret savored mostly in the mind. What of it is real? The mockingbirds

bicker in the fig tree, and the jays scold and hiss, but they've ceased to sing before I'm done

hearing the note. We build our impressions from the scattered sticks of lost afternoons,

one minute raised from the wreckage of the last. The sky and the landmarks we've learned

look innocent enough, but they're a front for all we thought we'd buried by simply outliving it.

There's something painful pooled in the furrows and drainage cuts, heaving up the sidewalks

and blacktop. The past is crowding against every bit of news. Take the smell of that lawn, mown

this morning to a uniform height, cut too close from the look of it—what comes into my head

is four decades done. If I had the time or the inclination to look more closely, it's possible

I could find something of beauty, something unremembered and immediate. But nature's peace

is a worrisome thing, an itch turning my mind from the task at hand, so much information

encoded on the back of the wind, brought forth in the quality of the day's duplicitous light.

Real Estate

After we closed on the house, I hurried to get it painted, late into the
    nights

for as long as I could keep going, tape and mud, cut in and roll. The
    rooms

were as big as they would ever be, emptied of furniture, the house open,
    unresolved.

Now we had to live here. I broke free the sashes, cross ventilation
    exchanging

paint fumes for city air. It was so quiet with the central unit shut down
    that I could hear

the erasable sounds the storm windows usually wouldn't admit, urban
    murmurings

more peaceful than I had expected, now and then a single sound
    emerging: somewhere

a car door slam and a kind of laughter, a freight train laboring on the
    L&N tracks

as mournful in town as it had ever sounded in the country, ambulances
    running

every red light on Poplar Avenue all the way to the Med, and then the
    close whisper

of my three-inch brush drawing a line along the molding's reveal,
    feathering it

down the wall in the echoing rooms we called our own. But ownership is
    the last lie

we tell ourselves—nothing goes unshared. Each eighth-of-an-acre parcel
    has belonged

to someone else and will again before long. The only thing approaching
    possession

is in the careful repairs we might make, every surface prepped and
    perfect, two coats

of ceiling white, eggshell and semi-gloss for the walls and trim, clear poly curing

on the oak floors, bleach searing the grout of the bathroom tiles, ammonia to polish

the lights of the old chandelier. Here in the heart of the city where nothing is new

we must make it so. On the last night before move-in I get to the closets. 220-grit paper

in a palm sander to take off just a little of the cedar, and there it is, like a liquor's bouquet,

a whisper of sharp cedar scent let loose from compartments in the wood's red grain.

Regarding Change

Front coming through. Even I can tell that. The air is unstable, like a stutter, like a sound made

to reach for and still push away the next sound. I can give the air a story—it is reluctant to move

and can't sit still. I can give the air its color—the viscous gray of wallpaper sizing trying to keep a slight shine

as it dries. Even a taste—like metal, like an old copper coin. But I wouldn't have understood it

the way my father did, sitting in the carport before supper, the knot of his tie yanked loose, watching the weather

come on. Decades removed from a Depression-era childhood, he still had a farmer's feel for the clouds

left over from a time when he would go to sleep to the rain's ringing on corrugated metal, the sound of the wind

in the battens and tarpaper, a sharecropper's son's certainty of bad luck and endless debt pulled around him

like a nine-patch quilt. And when the clouds piled high enough, not a lot could be said to have changed,

even in our tight suburban house, insulated by time, the sheets of rain hardly heard raking down the roof.

Fence Story

Almost anything can be bent into an explanation. On the drive, no one said a word

as the car shuddered over potholes the county crew couldn't keep filled, the road

a patchwork of hot mix aged to differing qualities of gray, the mendings themselves

as raised and rough as scabs, little better than what they sought to repair. The jack rattled

in the trunk behind me. Just an evening everyone else has forgotten, invited to dinner

at Arley Berry's house, the retired schoolteacher my father liked so much, eight miles

out in the country from our country town. He'd taught chemistry at the high school

since before there was chemistry. I was the kind of child you could take to eat

with old people: I listened, but didn't yet know what I was listening for. My father

missed the country ways he'd left in his childhood and believed they might make him

happy again. He would've moved us out here if he ever thought of a way. So much

easier to yearn for any past thing—the Great Depression, say, or a hard day driving

a team of mules, the plow upending rows of gray earth—than to come to terms with

the single hour you're in. Though my mother always emphasized how important it was

to reciprocate, they were never invited to our house. After supper that night we went out to look over the property, the vegetable garden and peach orchard,

cows gaping at us from the other side of the fence, slack barbwire stapled

to knotty posts, the whole bucolic scene struggling to emerge from the edgeless light

that gets associated with memory. I believed I could hear the hum of the current

shot into the one light-gauge wire without barbs, stretched new and taut

between yellow insulators. I had only thought about reaching for it. "That fence

will knock you down if you touch it, son." My mother had been left inside

to talk to Mrs. Berry. What about, I couldn't guess. "She'll have no part

of living in the country," I'd already heard my father say. Arley Berry was opening

the blade of his penknife and wrapping the bone handle in a doubled-up handkerchief.

"You don't need to do that," my father told him, never one for pointless show.

"The boy wants to see." Arley Berry was a teacher, there was no denying that. I remember

the sparks coming off the wire, hyphen shaped and angered. No, *angered* isn't right—

the sparks were relieved, sprung into the still air like water from a hose. Just a touch

of the knife blade's carbon steel was all it took. I suppose you could say

such a thing was beautiful, segmented sparks perfectly white in the perfectly still

gloaming, something so pure it left a stain across the dusty shadows, a spectacle

that might catch in a boy's memory to be wrenched wordward these years
   later, so long

since I have come to understand a thing or two about what it's best to
   never touch

and the kind of marks that might be burnt into the evening's draperied
   light if you do.

Piece of Memory

At the state line the road changed. Narrow, shoulderless Kentucky highway
    broadened

to wheel tax-subsidized Tennessee roads, only two lanes of blacktop, but wider
    and welcoming,

as if they had a mind to show you something. If this isn't my earliest memory, it's
    close to it.

I was still thinking about how the movers had taken down the television antenna
    at the old house

that morning and lain it tenderly in the yard. Even memory can't rid itself of
    memory, some glinting

splinter of before. Our stories get built up like a muddy delta rising from the Gulf,
    all night long

the spent river letting loose its sediments. I like to think this memory is of the
    trip we made

when we moved back to Tennessee for good, but it could have been any of the
    drives

home to visit family, or a dream of them pieced from whatever's come to hand.
    Most knowledge

is collage. Who knows why we keep what we keep? After lunch that day we were
    held up

by a freight train dragging itself southerly home, the highway crooked upward to
    a single set

of tracks. And this: through the empty boxcars I could see squared segments of
    Tennessee sky—

blue freight marbled with cirrus and frailly translucent as bone china, made of
    the same blue, really,

as what I'd left behind, but framed like that in the opened doors of the boxcars, it
    was easy to believe

the sky held a new promise lent by the tree-strewn country it shuttled over. After
    the train had passed,

the lights of the warning signal still ticked on and off, persisting for a handful of
beats even after

the rust-scarred caboose cleared the crossing and moved on down the line to
Hazel and Paris,

flat grades and trestles over poorly drained bottomland, and then the junction at
Jackson, Tennessee.

Essay on Sources

All art is folk art, made with whatever is at hand and bound up
with an adhesive of faith. I'll tell you about my materials, old words
seemingly naive and guileless as squares of fabric pulled blind
from the remnant bag, colorfast but weathered to a tender hand, each one
with a private and storied former life, a history of intimate touch,
pieces of Sunday finery and work clothes now shredded and waiting
to be put to some next use, vocabulary of old silk and satin, logic
of flannel and cotton duck, fine-wale corduroy worn flat and shiny.
My grammar has the feel of old twine, a simple ligature improvised
of necessity, the way old 280-thread-count bed linens may be torn
into strips and used to tie tomato vines to the stake, hoisting
their sagging limbs so each fruit stays clear of the ruinous ground.
What is there to make with old things, these sad discardings
of spendthrift forebears? Even the thoughts in my head come secondhand,
like beams and plank siding torn from a fallen-in barn. The few things
I believe are as old as the spalted wood that has survived dry rot
and termites, oak and old-growth pine tested and cured, pierced
with square nails, some still bent and hidden in the tight grain, waiting
to ruin a saw blade, or gap the iron in the plane that tries to reshape them.
My sentences may as well be made with the old tools, beech-handled fluting gouges
and mortise chisels, my grandfather's #5 jack plane come down to me
the same as my eye color and the pronunciation of certain diphthongs.
Any good tool will return to sharp if you hone it. Salvage and repair
should be the work of all saying, finding a way to use used things. Sometimes
the wear on a word makes it mean more, gives it a color slightly shifted
into newness. I am left with the words from my grandmother's mouth,

some of them as inscrutable as a line of untranslated Chaucer. I have never heard
a new word. All the words I know how to say have a warp or crimp bitten
into them by the people who came before me. I pick them up and secret them
into my pocket like mercury dimes or wheat pennies, like the broomcorn straw
left here and there on the gray porch boards after the morning sweeping.

The Mind of the Poet

When there was habitat enough—and quail—you could just about train
   a dog

in the field. Point, back, retrieve. It was all one elegant game for the
   setters

my father raised during those years, bred to a perfect simplicity. No
   matter

how long I'd been away, the only thing it was allowed to talk
   about

while we were hunting was hunting. And dogs. *Tekoa Mountain
   Sunrise*

*puts a lot of leg in a dog. A good setter'll hunt nice and close. Wasn't no
   breaking*

that heavy-mouthed pointer. While we cradled our firearms, their ribbed
   barrels

kept more or less skyward, and stepped delicately over the just-thawed
   ground

as Bunny and Charlie swung out on another long cast, my father might go
   into

the workings of the bird dog mind, how it gets arrested in its
   development—

retarded was the word he used—"They have only one love, the good ones
   do,

just the hunting makes any sense to their bird dog brains, just the one
   game

over and over." We stood at the high end of the field and watched the
   dogs

working the edges, so careful and relentless: so *glad*. "They'll hunt in their
   sleep,"

he would say admiringly. Once, toward the end of the season, when I came
   back

from walking the dogs to the pen, he nodded down Manley Street and
    told me how

Swats Scarborough and a little pointer bitch got up ten coveys over that
    piece of ground

the day before he had to leave for World War II. There was always a
    story,

and I sometimes believed he had us hunt just so he could tell it. Manley
    Street

was ranch houses and rusted swing sets, as far as I was concerned, and
    always had been,

nut grass and ground ivy choking the Bermuda. It's been years since you
    could hear

a quail whistle this close to town. Every now and again when I'm
    driving up home

I'll see a chain-link kennel behind an old farmhouse on Highway 79, an
    arbor of pines

throwing late shade on a liver-spotted pointer fluidly pacing, lost in a
    dream

of opening day. From the breadth of her chest, a real field splitter. Such
    waste

is always beautiful, I guess, but it breaks my heart to see them raise their
    heads,

testing at the wind, off-season fat but ready to lock into a point, so
    purified

and undistractable, going about their olden art on the kennel's concrete
    slab, playing

a game so much larger than the dimensions of a pent life, this strange
    pastime

that no longer matters at all, hunting what has turned to story and left
    here for good.

A Student's Notes: Marseilles, Christmas 1986

We sat in the doorway of a butcher shop and waited out the day,

the midmorning sky an unhelpful scrim of white, cold and
  depthless,

too bright to look to for any direction. We knew where the sea was,

just down the street of closed cafés, and the wind wrote *north* on the
  side

of our faces, reproaching us, I thought, for being there in the Old Port at
  all

with no place to go. Christmas was just another day in the youth
  hostel:

kicked out by ten, the doors locked until five. I knew it would be like
  this.

I had come to Europe to learn something, I'm not sure what.
  Anyway,

it was what one did. Go while you're a student. You appreciate
  nothing

until you've stood in the cathedrals. But on that day I was thankful

for a good pair of boots and a warm coat. I'd left my gloves in a taxi

the night before, after midnight mass at Notre Dame de la Garde, and my
  hands

were scalded by the raw wind. We'd stood with the reverent fishermen
  and sung

the familiar carols in not so familiar French, me, my friend Chris, some
  kid

from Holland, and the Oxford student we couldn't get rid of. It was all
  too strange

to make me homesick. One way to think about it is to say I lost
  everything

that bitter day in Marseilles. If the point of education is to give you a
  word

for the things that will be torn from you, I had some lessons yet to
   learn.

My innocence was still a hard place inside me like a knot in a slab of yellow
   pine—

hit it the wrong way with the saw and the whole board would split down the
   grain.

Later that afternoon I called home from a coin phone. My brother picked
   up,

just in from Dallas. I could hear voices in the background, my family in a
   stifling kitchen

beginning their Christmas, and yes, they all sounded far away. From where
   I spoke

I could see French kids riding their new bicycles. Two guys in skin suits
   paddled

their surfboards into the waves. It occurred to me there is really little
   difference

between one place and another. That evening we found our way back to
   shelter, thankful

to have a bed, but the very idea of shelter felt like a lie, and I found myself
   preferring

the cold stone step of the butcher shop, the sun's truthful disregard.
   Honesty

is hard to come by, even in the weather. The luminous dial of my watch
   comforted me

in the dark as it broke the night into exact parts, the wait for daylight easier
   to take

once I could see it so evenly cut. But let's not leave it there. Some weeks later,

when I was home in Tennessee, my mother introduced me to a distant
   relation we ran into

in a catfish restaurant. He was in the produce business. To be polite he
   asked me

what I'd thought about the things I'd seen while I'd been away, and I told
   him

about the fruit I'd eaten in the middle of winter in France. "Best in the
   world,"

he said, "grown in North Africa." Amid all the cathedrals and paintings,
   the Gare d'Orsay

and Shakespeare & Company, all the cold blank days, I remembered the
   fruit, a tangerine

I bought in Toulouse or Aix. When I pulled it apart, there was a hidden
   section embraced

by all the others, what I later learned was called the kiss, waiting for me
   perfect and sweet.

Jerry Lee Lewis Plays "That Lucky Old Sun" at Bad Bob's Vapors Club, Memphis, Tennessee

I'll tell it if you let me, my story of those nights we spent watching the Killer
    play

a smoky room down on Brooks Road, almost to State Line. Can't you hear
    the note

of reverence in my voice, the sweet pity of tragedy? Even when he wasn't half
    trying,

the songs fell from his lips so sorrow-encrusted and smoldering, so flavorful
    I'd swear

they'd been basketed from the roiling grease of a deep fryer, his offhand
    rendering

of "That Lucky Old Sun" owing nothing to Ray Charles, and everything.
    Show me

that river . . . take me across. There was an inwardness to how he spoke the
    song, owning

the piece for just that moment, his leaning over to tell the microphone what
    he had to tell it

so personal an act we were almost shamed by our fascination. The song's a
    prayer,

another brief hymn to the emptiness inside us and what we hope might
    come

to fill it. On the piano a cigar was cocked and cold in the ashtray, waiting to
    be relit

when the song was done. Just a night of sight-seeing, September 1988, gone
    slumming

to hear the great and forgotten, none of us quite young enough to be young
    anymore.

The Vapors Club was exactly what you're imagining, show starts at ten, five
    dollar cover

at the door. The gray-blue light, where there was light, had grown so stale and clouded

it seemed to have clabbered, and even the shadows in the shadowy room were bowed

with the weight of something I didn't have a name for. The regulars bore it like soldiers—

paying customers flammable with hairspray and spent chances, slickened with a whiskey glow,

Ten High bourbon redistilled through their pores, sugary and volatile. Everyone in the place

had twenty years and a marriage or two on me. They'd lost something time took, the edges

of experience as fine and full of meaning as the cuttings in the grooves of an LP record

played too many times on a console stereo in the living room, a diamond stylus harrowing

its windy memory from the satiny grooves. I was just learning to love, tallying what cost

to lose myself as one long breath into another person, not knowing what would be left of me

once I was drawn back into myself. There is a point past which we will never again be able

to call ourselves detached, but on that night it was just music, a man punishing a piano

for wanting to keep something clenched in the tension of its iron harp, just a few hours

taking us toward another night's savory fatigue and upending, the insects' pulsed cries measuring

what was left of the year's heat, parking lot gravel crunching underfoot, then the car bounding

over the curb back onto Brooks Road, the bar smells we would wear for awhile, dance sweat

and menthol 100s, hair spray and Kiwi shoe polish, spray-on perfume. Then
the driving

back to Midtown and our own shabby rooms, the car windows down, details
of the skyline

edge-etched to the windshield, unheavened, sense-bound, all of us silent and
rehearsing

our arrangement of the night's sharps and flats, a version shaped to suit our
own dying voices.

ACKNOWLEDGMENTS

Several of these poems, some in earlier versions, appeared in the following publications: *Agni Online, Basilica Review, Cimarron Review, Clackamas Literary Review, Columbia Poetry Review, Connecticut Review, Epoch, Georgia Review, Greensboro Review, Grist, Image, Iron Horse Literary Review, Literary Review, Marlboro Review, Meridian, New Millennium Writings, River City, Shenandoah, Southern Humanities Review, Southern Review, Southwest Review,* and *Sou'wester.*

"New Bill Meyer Stadium," which originally appeared in *Shenandoah,* has been anthologized in *Knoxville Bound: A Collection of Literary Works Inspired by Knoxville, Tennessee* (2004). "Paper Anniversary," which originally appeared in *Southwest Review,* was featured on *Poetry Daily.* "Piece of Memory" was published in *Outscape: Writings on Fences and Frontiers* (2008).

Marilyn Kallet is to blame for all this. I would also like to thank my wife, to whom this small book is dedicated; my children, Callaway and Emmaline; and the rest of my far-flung family and friends for years of indulgence and love. My students and colleagues at Union University continue to make my day job a pleasure. My own teachers—Charles, Greg, George, John—set high standards for the work and the life. The Pew Charitable Trusts provided a generous grant that assisted in the writing of several of these poems. A research leave from Union University and residencies at the Virginia Center for the Creative Arts provided needed time to complete the manuscript.